LITTLE LESSONS OF
LOVE

LITTLE LESSONS OF

LOVE

Elizabeth Heller

With a foreword by David Heller, Ph.D.

Conari Press
Berkeley, CA

Conari Press books are distributed by Publishers Group West.

Printed in the United States of America on recycled paper.

ISBN 0-943233-73-9

Cover design and illustration: Christine Leonard Raquepaw

Library of Congress Cataloging-in-Publication Data

Heller, Elizabeth
    Little lessons of love / Elizabeth Heller ; with an introduction
by David Heller.
            p.   cm.
    ISBN 0-943233-73-9 (trade paper) : $8.95

    1. Love—United States— Public Opinion.

    2. Public Opinion—United States.   I. Title.

BF575.L8H379   1994
152.4"1—dc20   94-28892

10 9 8 7 6 5 4 3 2 1

For Little Mookie

Where there is love there is hope,
Where there is hope there is faith,
And where there is faith, all things are possible.

ACKNOWLEDGMENTS

To all the generous adults and children
who so graciously shared their experiences and their
wisdom about love to make this book possible.
To my editor, Mary Jane Ryan,
for her support and faith in this project.
To Will Glennon and the staff at Conari Press.
And especially to my husband, David,
for the little lessons of love he shares with me each day.
I offer you all, my heartfelt thanks.

TABLE OF CONTENTS

FOREWORD

While considering how to introduce this captivating collection on love, I am reminded of the words of the psychologist Erich Fromm, who wrote: "Love is an act of faith, and whoever is of little faith is also of little love." There is something inherently spiritual about *Little Lessons of Love,* for it offers to all of us a compelling and practical philosophy of love, full of the elements of faith, with which we can enhance our own love relationships.

Perhaps this helpful spirituality should not come as a surprise, given the fresh, down-to-earth, and beautifully simple format of the book. Real people talking about their real-life experiences with love and generously offering guidance to the rest of us—there's something universally appealing and uplifting about that process in itself. The many spontaneous yet profound sayings that emerge from these pages are a testament to the considerable vision we can find in our own hearts, if only we summon the confidence and courage to explore. For in our own hearts lie the deepest and most profound answers to the questions of love, and how love is related to the stars above and the world of the Spirit that we cannot see but can only feel.

Among the hundreds of wise aphorisms included in this book, I find myself drawn in particular to those that summarize love in just a few brief, cogent words, such as the thoughtful observations of Ginny, age seventy-one, who shared: "Love comes to those who tend their inner garden . . . for them, love is sure to bloom." How thought-provoking such comments are, and how they beckon further reflection. It is our natural desire and really our obligation to reflect on love's ways, for such consideration can only deepen our capacity for love. As well as words can capture, the moving wisdom in this fine collection, concerned variously with the origins of love, our dating and romantic mores, marriage, and the course and meaning of love, nobly elevates our thinking and tugs at our hearts in a manner befitting the subject that can only be described as inspirational.

Love is truly inescapable. It's a major part of the reason we are here on earth, and, truth be told, most of us would have it no other way. Nevertheless, we do encounter difficulties and frustrations in our love relationships, sometimes due to circumstances that mystify us. I strongly believe that this book will help people with such problems and offer new perspectives on something as essential to us as the air we breathe and the water we drink.

May you discover the great joy and understanding that is revealed in this thoughtful book, and may you come to know love more intimately in your own life. Together we gladly seek the nature of love, that glad taste of heaven that we may experience right here in our everyday lives.

David Heller, Ph.D.
author of *Love Is Like A Crayon,
Because It Comes In All Colors*

INTRODUCTION

It is my ardent belief that the greatest thing we can do for ourselves and for humanity is to learn how to love. Throughout my own life I have found that the great philosophers and teachers of love are not found only in books, they are the strangers who ride the subway with us to work, the children who play in the school yard, the husbands or wives we come home to each night. Each of us has something profound to offer about love.

Through triumph and through painful experiences, we collect knowledge in our hearts and wisdom in our souls concerning love. We share some of those truths with friends and significant others all the time. But what if a person in Vermont were to share his or her wisdom with a stranger in California? The idea of gathering this collective wisdom so that people who don't know each other can reach out and teach each other something about love is what inspired me to create this book.

As with many challenges in life, I embarked on this literary journey with my own preconceived curiosities and notions about love in mind. But, as the philosopher Martin Buber said, "Every journey has a secret destination." As I began speaking with the more than 150 interviewees, I realized that I was not traveling alone, but instead was heading in the same direction as each and every person I interviewed. We were all curious about the many facets of love and in some way were searching for love's answers. I had not anticipated that there would be such a profound connectedness among our journeys, and I hope you will experience that too as you read this book.

With great enthusiasm and generosity, each of my interviewees young and old, single or engaged, married or divorced, offered touching thoughts and often whimsical quips about love. Whether age eight or eighty-two, people consistently remarked that they had never really asked themselves such direct questions about love. But when they were provided with the encouragement to reflect on love, my interviewees responded with a wealth of understanding, insight, and humor. Many people I spoke with were pleasantly surprised at how much firsthand knowledge about love they possessed, and this was one of the most rewarding aspects of the project for me.

We cannot begin to understand life's answers unless we are first willing to ask ourselves important questions about love. So along with all the wonderful people who made this book possible, I invite you not only to take in their wisdom, but to find your own along the way. It is my pleasure to share this compendium about love from people representing many different backgrounds, religious viewpoints, and walks of life. It is my deepest desire that somewhere in this book, one or many of the quotations will speak to you personally, a comment, a sentence, a thought that touches your heart and somehow seems meant just for you.

Elizabeth Heller

CHAPTER I

THE SEEDS OF LOVE

"Love is the enchanted dawn of every heart."
—Alphonse De Lamartine

To think about love is to feel a lightness come over one's heart. But while taking in love's freshness and glory, have you ever stopped to wonder where love comes from and how it comes to be?

Among the many journeys of life, we all have one journey in common—the heartfelt yearning and search for love. From the time we are born until the time we pass on, we spend our most profound moments in awe, in pain, in hopefulness, and in joy over love.

The quest for love seems as much a part of our nature as using our feet to run or our minds to think. As children, love is a hug from our parents or a secret note passed to us in school from our best friend. As adolescents, love takes on greater dimension: learning to love yourself, dating, the first kiss, a breakup, learning to risk again. As adults, we experience the depth of love: searching for love, struggling with commitment, and then ultimately finding a lasting love. But whether a child or a grandparent, rich or poor, married or single, we each seem to be longing for love to fill our hearts.

While you are considering the nature and origin of love, also consider this: Perhaps the answers to love's questions are already within your heart. So enjoy and learn from what people of all ages have said about love, but also pay proper respect and listen closely to your own feelings, for they have much to teach you as well.

WHAT DOES LOVE DO FOR YOU?

"Love helps you see with your heart as well as your eyes."
   Liz, 29

♥

"Love ought to be good for hiccups because it scares most people to death."
   Randall, 25

♥

"Love gives you the courage of a lion and the gentleness of a lamb."
   Joseph, 47

♥

"Love gives you faith that life is more than we know."
   Hank, 65

♥

"Love puts extra sugar in your morning coffee."
   Sandra, 22

"Love puts a glow on your cheeks, so you don't have to spend so much money on blush."
Anna, 17

♥

"It's supposed to make you feel like a kid again . . . But I'm not sure why."
Kirsten, 9

♥

"Love gives you a renewed sense of hope that today will be better than yesterday."
Julie, 34

♥

"To love is to know the ecstasy of human existence."
Matthew, 80

♥

"It gives you someone to buy chocolates for on Valentine's Day."
Gina, 9

"Love gives you the best reason not to watch television in the evening."
Jenna, 29

♥

"Love may not be the answer for everything, but it can help you remember what the questions are."
Abby, 26

♥

"Love lets you view the world with hope, promise, and faith."
Caroline, 29

♥

"It provides you with a companion for many things and yet reminds you about what a unique individual you really are."
Dean, 40

♥

"Love heals the past and paints rainbows for the future."
Betty, 47

WHAT IS THE SOURCE OF ALL LOVE?

"Love gives you somebody who keeps all your secrets locked safely in their heart."
   Jennifer, 12

♥

"Imagination . . . You can love as passionately and fervently as your imagination allows."
   Helen, 42

♥

"It comes from a wellspring inside our souls. But to find the wellspring, you have to be willing to search your heart."
   Brian, 29

♥

"The source of all love is like a river overflowing with fish—once you throw in your line, you're guaranteed a big catch."
   Billy, 45

7

"Love is made in a factory shaped like a heart, and the workers give it away for free."
   Gina, 7

♥

"You can't search for love; love comes to you when you take a rest from searching."
   Jason, 29

♥

"Love must flow from somewhere; every stream has a beginning."
   Adelle, 30

♥

"Faith . . . You gotta believe there is something richer than riches and more powerful than possessions."
   David, 35

♥

"Love comes from your family. You bring it with you in life and look for it from other people, too."
   Catherine, 28

"The source of all love is like a big, pink grapefruit—you have to work to squeeze the juice out of it."

Mike, 18

♥

"Love grows out of people's need to nurture and care. It starts as a selfish thing and ends up a selfless one."

Debra, 38

♥

"It's like my wonderful Italian grandmother when she serves dinner: No matter how much love we have already taken in, the Source insists there's always room for another helping."

Marie, 30

♥

"We have the power within ourselves to create love or to create friction—the choice is ours."

George, 41

♥

"My heart knows all love comes from God."

Ginny, 7

WHY DOES EVERYONE NEED LOVE?

"In the end, all we can do on earth is love . . .
Love teaches us that love is its own reward."
   Chad, 58

♥

"Love is the lamp inside your heart—it keeps
you from tripping in the dark."
   Caroline, 30

♥

"The ability to love is the most valuable thing a
person can own."
   Irene, 60

♥

"You need love to keep the smiles coming."
   Kevin, 9

♥

"Love makes your sniffles go away."
   Kari, 7

"We need love because love is the great healer, and we all have wounds that need mending."
Brenda, 29

♥

"Love invariably brings out the real you."
David, 35

♥

"Love is the meat and potatoes of living, while happiness is the wine, and joy is the dessert."
Liz, 29

♥

"If you are living without love in your life, your zip code might as well be 00000."
Kim, 20

♥

"Needing love is as practical in life as needing a cotton sweater: It keeps you warm in the winter and cool in the summer and shrinks only if you don't take proper care of it."
Nellie, 82

How do we fall in love?

"That's the greatest mystery of all time. I don't know how an airplane flies either, but I get on and enjoy the ride anyway."
George, 41

♥

"You fall in love when you find someone who might bring you breakfast in bed."
Amy, 24

♥

"Common interests and uncommon looks."
Wendy, 29

♥

"To fall in love, the stars have to be in the right place, and then again, so do you."
Margaret, 32

"Falling in love is as easy as baking a cake—if you don't slam the oven door, things will heat up nicely."

Elyse, 49

♥

"I haven't figured out falling in love yet. I'm still working on not falling when I ice skate."

Terri, 8

♥

"You fall in love in a genuine way when the passion part of you and the practical part of you elect to make a go of it together."

Daphne, 42

♥

"It's like a secret rendezvous that neither party planned on but both are mighty glad they attended."

Sarah, 30

"It really isn't that hard to fall in love. It just takes a mooshy attitude."
     Lina, 8

♥

"Falling in love is like tripping and forgetting to get up on your feet before it's too late."
     Mike, 18

♥

"God is a part-time matchmaker."
     Betty, 47

WHAT ROLE DO LOOKS PLAY WHEN IT COMES TO FALLING IN LOVE?

"To begin with, love gets people all red in the face."

Adam, 8

♥

"It's the fuel that gets your engine going . . . But if that's all there is, the relationship will eventually run out of gas."

George, 41

♥

"A caring person looks more beautiful the longer you are with them."

Denise, 33

♥

"A shapely body doesn't tell you much about the shape of a person's character."

Lydia, 43

"When you're both seventy, you could well forget what you both looked like when you were twenty . . . But you'll never forget what you said to each other."
Roselyn, 40

♥

"Keep looking and you will find a blemish; keep understanding and you will find a lover and a friend."
Vivian, 38

♥

"Whoever you are in love with always seems to be the most beautiful person in the world."
Mike, 18

♥

"A good sense of humor makes anyone beautiful."
Marci, 20

"A person's true beauty is revealed over time . . . You can't expect to know all you need to know at a glance."
Pat, 52

♥

"Beauty is a big deal until you find out you aren't perfect either . . . Then it's not such a big deal after all."
Fred, 39

♥

"The story of Beauty and the Beast says it all— a little love can turn any relationship into a fairy tale."
Liz, 29

How can you tell when someone has inner beauty?

"How generous are they? That question will give you the clearest answer."
Laura, 18

♥

"It's like a magnet—your heart is instantly drawn toward theirs."
Noah, 36

♥

"Just ask them. If they are telling the truth, then they have inner beauty."
Lisette, 10

"Inner beauty comes from a person's goodness, morals, ethics, and intrinsic beliefs. It's an aura—it glows."
   Debra, 38

♥

"You see it in a person's eyes, in their smile. It's when a person is genuine."
   Stacie, 24

♥

"When you find yourself being attracted to a person's warmth and spirit—not just their legs."
   Matthew, 47

♥

"If a person is more concerned about the welfare of others than about themselves, they definitely have inner beauty."
   Catherine, 28

"Being pretty on the inside means you don't hit your brother and you eat all your peas—that's what my Grandma taught me."
Jennie, 7

♥

"Inner beauty comes from inner peace and a deep comfort with who you are."
Roselyn, 75

♥

"Someone with inner beauty makes you feel like sunshine just flooded the room."
Dean, 50

♥

"Inner beauty . . . That's God's way of showing us that we can all make a difference through who we are on the inside, no matter what physical imperfections we might have on the outside."
Liza, 31

HOW CAN YOU BECOME A MORE LOVING PERSON?

"Instead of judging other people, try to understand them."
Cassie, 30

♥

"Be more accepting of faults—especially those that you possess yourself."
Mike, 18

♥

"Be willing to give more than you get back."
Catherine, 28

♥

"You can start with common courtesy—returning someone's phone call or the hedge clippers you borrowed can be a powerful gesture of kindness."
Silvia, 45

"Love yourself . . . the more self-love you have, the more love there is to give to others."
   Nat, 47

♥

"Hang a giant heart from your roof to let everyone know you are friendly. It might even catch on in your neighborhood."
   Haley, 7

♥

"Be forgiving toward the world in general— share your love, not your anger."
   Al, 29

♥

"Reevaluate your goals . . . be sure you are motivated by generosity and not greed."
   Phil, 55

♥

"Listen better, try harder, give more."
   Scott, 24

"Next time a homeless person asks you for money, buy them something to eat."
Dick, 40

♥

"Have faith in God, have faith in yourself, and have faith in the goodness of others."
Ginny, 71

♥

"Be generous with your wisdom. We all know things that can help others on their journey through life."
Vivian, 38

WHAT IS THE RELATIONSHIP BETWEEN LOVE AND FRIENDSHIP?

"At the end of our marriage ceremony the rabbi said: 'May you be friends for life.' That says it all."

Ilene, 40

♥

"Friendship is to love what water is to a flower: Friendship gives love a chance to bloom."

Stella, 63

♥

"Love and friendship are brothers, but love is the more hot-blooded of the two."

Dean, 50

"Real love lasts because the friendship is never over."
Stacie, 24

♥

"Love and friendship are like cookies and milk—they are at their best when they are together."
Liz, 29

♥

"Finding true love is like finding a long-lost friend . . . Once you are together, you feel like there was never a time when you were apart."
Marissa, 30

♥

"They're pretty similar, because from what I've seen, both friends and lovers have trouble saying good-bye to each other."
Ginger, 9

"The goal of all love is for a lover to be your best friend, and continue to be your lover just the same."
David, 35

♥

"You have to plant the seeds of friendship in order to find a harvest of love."
Sarah, 39

♥

"They're like roommates—you can't visit one without bumping into the other."
Derek, 41

How do you know when it is genuine love and not infatuation?

"When you can lounge around together in your old clothes and still feel as attracted to each other as when you're dressed for a night on the town."

Bret, 36

♥

"You know it's real love when you've been at it for thirty years."

David, 35

♥

"It might be real love when you stop giggling and have a big smile on your face instead."

Terrance, 8

♥

"When you can't imagine your life without your lover in it, then it's true love."

Carl, 42

"Infatuation is like a rose—it's beautiful but it dies quickly. Love is like an oak tree—it grows strong roots, changes with the seasons, and always flourishes again."
Liz, 29

♥

"You can tell it's real love by time . . . Infatuation is short-lived; love is eternal."
Scott, 24

♥

"Infatuation is like being in a candy store and wanting everything you see. Love is like being in a candy store and wanting only your favorite jelly beans for the rest of your life."
Anita, 44

♥

"Infatuation is sex and physicality. Love is when you get that wonderful queasy feeling in your stomach."
Stacie, 24

"If it's love, you see the other person as they really are, with all their faults and imperfections, and that's acceptable to you. With infatuation, your vision is distorted and you see the other person as perfect."
　　Debra, 38

♥

"Real love is something you realize over time. Infatuation is when you are more in love with the idea of love than with the person."
　　Catherine, 28

♥

"It is like the saying 'practice makes perfect': Infatuation is the act of practicing love, and real love is perfecting your ability to care about another."
　　Hank, 65

Love comes to those who . . .

"Date."
    Debra, 39

♥

"Don't sit around waiting for it to come to them."
    Daphne, 42

♥

"Aren't afraid to dive off the diving board in the deep end of the pool . . . That's how I met my boyfriend."
    Sheila, 11

♥

"Love comes to women who like sports—those women have men all figured out."
    Frankie, 20

"Love comes to everybody at one time or another."

Blanche, 70

♥

"Tend their inner garden—for them love is sure to bloom."

Ginny, 71

♥

"Love comes to girls who like spiders—that way you can be sure they won't scream when you show them your bug collection."

Geoffrey, 9

♥

"Love comes to the plain and the beautiful, the tall and the short, the fat and the thin . . . It comes to everybody who is ready for it."

Karl, 44

"Understand that finding love is like buying a house . . . you have a list of things you want, but once you find one you really like, you may have to compromise on a few of the amenities so you can move in."

A.C., 38

♥

"Those who are more interested in dialogue than diamonds."

Ann Mary, 43

CHAPTER II

PARTNERS IN LOVE

"Love is friendship set on fire."
—Jeremy Taylor

erhaps one of life's most rewarding and yet challenging experiences is looking for a partner for life, a soul-mate. What drives this quest is a desire to be deeply connected to another human being in the bond of heartfelt love. We want to know the joy of caring, sharing, and growing with another. We hope for the security of faithful love waiting for us at the end of each day and at the beginning of the next. Finding a partner can give us "a wonderful queasy feeling in our stomachs" and the solid courage to fulfill our dreams.

The popular romantic elements—candlelight, flowers, and chocolates—all may enhance a court-ship and set the stage for love. But the question many people want answered is how to find that very special someone.

When your heart tells you one thing and your head tells you another, to which do you listen? How can you help someone fall in love with you? Can there be more than one "Mr. or Ms. Right"?

These are all questions that captivate us and beckon for thoughtful consideration.

As you move toward adding romance in your life, or if you are already on a romantic path, seek the knowledge of others and take heart, for someone else's heart is surely ready to take in yours. As we learn throughout our relationships, those that are fleeting as well as those that endure, "it is a beautiful necessity of our nature to love" (Douglas Jerrold). We can all be thankful for that great and profound need.

WHAT SHOULD YOU LOOK FOR IN A SOULMATE?

"Eternal compatibility, or at least someone who doesn't hog the popcorn."
   Carina, 25

♥

"Someone with a good sense of humor and the ability to laugh at him or herself."
   Gene, 45

♥

"Search for someone who knows himself well."
   Catherine, 28

♥

"Someone with passion, compassion, and a good job."
   Ilene, 40

"Go after fantasy and you may never find love; love exists only in someone who is real."

Danny, 40

♥

"Look for someone who always sees the glass half-full then you're sure not to fall into a half-empty relationship."

Liz, 29

♥

"Look for a person who treats others with respect, gentleness, warmth, and, last but certainly not least, love itself."

Hank, 65

♥

"Someone with a positive attitude and happy outlook . . . . That kind of person has a contagious view of life you don't mind catching."

Ashley, 25

"Find a person who will lend you their crayons when yours break."
  Lucy, 8

♥

"Someone who thinks *home* and *hearth* are the two best words in life."
  David, 35

♥

"Find the person who has the key to your heart."
  Ginny, 71

♥

"Someone with a bicycle so you can travel places together."
  Cindi, 10

What kind of person should you avoid at all costs?

"A person who never combs their hair."
Lana, 10

♥

"Someone who tries to change you for their benefit."
Andrea, 24

♥

"People who constantly talk about their own needs and never ask about yours."
Melinda, 30

♥

"Anyone who makes you feel less than you are. If they leave you diminished as a person, you shouldn't be in the relationship."
Debra, 38

♥

"Someone with a big past and a dim future."
Stacie, 24

"The kind that are desperate to get married—you'll never have a chance to let your love grow because they'll always be rushing you along."

Vivian, 38

♥

"Men who want to get to know your body before they get to know you."

Ilene, 40

♥

"Materialism, if carried to excess, makes a poor bedfellow."

Eleanor, 48

♥

"Avoid insecure people who are looking to lean on you and looking for you to live their life for them."

Catherine, 28

♥

"If a person is more concerned about your appearance then your feelings, RUN!"

Liz, 29

ARE THERE MANY POTENTIAL LOVES IN THE COURSE OF A PERSON'S LIFE, OR JUST ONE SPECIAL SOULMATE?

"There might be a lot of them, but I think you are only allowed to have one."
Gretchen, 7

♥

"Finding a partner is like finding the final piece to a two-piece puzzle: You can try and squeeze pieces in, but there's only one perfect fit."
Bernadette, 29

♥

"There are many potential partners who might say 'I do,' but only one who will really mean it."
Hank, 65

"I believe there are many possible people for you, but each one is different. And if you find one that is true, by all means stay with her."
Scott, 24

♥

"If there's more than one right person for me, they must be an angel, because the one I have is already heaven-sent."
David, 35

♥

"It's like 'Let's Make A Deal': If you already have a good prize, you have to be careful—giving it up for what's behind 'door number two' or 'door number three' might leave you with nothing."
George, 41

♥

"For some there is one right person, and for others there are many possibilities. It depends on how much compatibility you want in your relationship."
Debra, 38

"You have to go through a lot of people to find the right one. It's like the saying 'You have to kiss a lot of toads to find the prince'."
    Catherine, 28

♥

"When someone is born, God makes sure there is just one special person matched up for them—it's like a continuation of Noah's Ark."
    Maryanne, 23

IS THERE A PERFECT TIME FOR FALLING IN LOVE?

"Fall in love when you fully love yourself. Then your relationship will be rich and fulfilling."

   Delia, 32

♥

"Don't do it in science class . . . The teacher may find your love note and read it to the whole class."

   Shea, 12

♥

"Love happens when you are ready for it . . . there's no age limit, no deadline, and it's not on any schedule."

   Catherine, 28

"Today, the present. But if not today, there's always tomorrow."
Janson, 46

♥

"Love can happen when you are close friends with someone and those feelings get deeper over time . . . until one day you realize you are already in love with them."
Andrea, 24

♥

"Love is at its best when you are at your best. Take care of yourself and love will take care of you."
Ken, 45

♥

"Don't worry about falling in love. When love is meant to be, it will happen."
Blanche, 70

"It's good to fall along with the leaves;
October's love will bring you together
 by the fire."
    Jake, 35

♥

"Sunset is very nice."
    Lucille, 55

♥

"The best time is anytime you least expect it."
    Carla, 20

♥

"The best time to fall in love is when the girl
has cable TV and you don't."
    Moe, 9

WHAT IS THE BEST WAY TO HELP SOMEONE FALL IN LOVE WITH YOU?

"Place it in Cupid's hands. . . . You can't force love."
　　Eleanor, 48

♥

"I suggest you give them a kiss at recess—but if you are under eight years old, it should be a chocolate kiss."
　　Marie Ann, 8

♥

"Like watering a thirsty plant, sprinkle your friendship with love."
　　Joan, 37

♥

"Don't hide your feelings—but do hide your dirty dishes."
　　Rob, 31

"You can't make someone fall in love with you.
Neither of you will be happy unless you come
to it yourselves."
    Heather, 22

♥

"It's the difference between a flashlight and a
searchlight—the brighter the love in your heart,
the more likely your love will be noticed."
    Raymond, 35

♥

"Make a fabulous dinner and invite them
over . . . It's especially good if it's spaghetti
or something else you can share off the
same plate."
    Margaret, 32

♥

"Falling in love is like parachuting—all you have
to do is have faith and let go."
    Efram, 38

WHAT SPECIAL QUALITIES DO YOU NEED IN ORDER TO BE A GOOD LOVER?

"A healing touch and a sensuous one, too."
  Morgan, 29

♥

"Know who you are and be happy with
  yourself."
  Stacie, 24

♥

"Sensible sensitivity."
  David, 35

♥

"Most good lovers like Chinese food . . .
Maybe eating with chopsticks makes you
more patient and deliberate."
  Robert, 34

"Don't take yourself too seriously, but always
take each other's feelings seriously."
  Liz, 29

♥

"Spontaneity, a sense of adventure, and
a deep sense of wanting to give pleasure
as well as receive it."
  Ken, 45

♥

"You've got to have enthusiasm."
  Debra, 38

♥

"Candlelight, satin sheets, and romantic music
can't take the place of true feelings of love—
if you have love, all you need is each other."
  Ryan, 54

♥

"You need to believe with your whole being
that love conquers all."
  Dolly, 56

"You have to have love in your heart
and passion in your soul."
  Alma, 30

♥

"You have to believe in magic."
  Vivian, 38

♥

"Flexibility—emotional flexibility, that is."
  Barbie, 35

WHAT KINDS OF THINGS ARE GOOD TO SAY WHEN YOU ARE IN LOVE?

"You mean so much to me."
   Ian, 35

♥

"True things, but not hurtful ones."
   Debra, 38

♥

"First of all, tell them you are in love with them—don't keep them guessing."
   Catherine, 28

♥

"Something romantic like 'Let's take a trailer and travel across the United States together'."
   Blanche, 70

"I think it's nice to say things like 'That ice-cream cone looks almost as good as you.'"
Donald, 10

♥

"Always say thank you, especially for little things like when your partner makes dinner or takes out the garbage. Everyone needs to feel appreciated."
Hank, 65

♥

"Be encouraging and say hopeful things. Be positive about life."
Ginny, 71

♥

"Be as attentive and courteous in your daily conversations as you were on your first date."
Liz, 29

♥

"You can never say enough 'I love you's."
Joseph, 47

"I love you, I support you, I need you."
    Scott, 24

♥

"How you listen is as important as what you
say. A good listener is a great communicator."
    John, 75

♥

"Always ask how your partner's day went
and be attentive—even if you've already
heard the story about the boss or the kids
a thousand times."
    Angela, 39

WHAT THINGS SHOULD YOU NEVER SAY TO YOUR PARTNER WHEN YOU'RE IN LOVE?

"Why are you wearing THAT?!"
Myra, 33

♥

"Never say 'I love you for your lunch snacks.'
That's how I lost my girlfriend."
Bryan, 8

♥

"Never compare them to someone else—
especially ex-lovers."
Catherine, 28

♥

"If you could only change this one thing about
yourself, that would be great."
Paula, 21

"Any derogatory remark like 'You owe me.'"
Scott, 24

♥

"Anything said in anger. You're liable to say things you don't mean and they can hit places you never aimed for."
Debra, 38

♥

"If you need to argue or discuss a problem, don't embarrass your partner by arguing in public. Head home or find some privacy."
Denise, 33

♥

"Physical appearance can be a touchy subject— never tell your partner they need to lose weight or change their hairstyle. Be encouraging and gentle instead."
Grant, 35

"Never put down your partner's accomplish-ments. Even if it seems minor to you, the accomplishment could be very significant to them."

George, 41

♥

"Don't say 'You're home so soon?!'"

Blanche, 70

♥

"How could you be so stupid!"

Stacie, 24

IS IT A GOOD IDEA TO SLEEP WITH SOMEONE BEFORE MARRIAGE?

"What's really the best idea is to love someone before marriage."
  Liz, 29

♥

"If you don't get married until your thirties or forties, then you're missing out on a lot of chances for growth."
  Stacie, 24

♥

"Yes, because the only thing more important than knowledge is self-knowledge."
  Marvin, 37

♥

"It doesn't hurt to give a person a test drive."
  Mike, 18

"Sex is the last step in a relationship. Commitment, love, and trust have to be there first. If those aren't there, it doesn't matter if you are married or not."
    Debra, 38

♥

"It's a good idea to wait until you're sure you are doing the right thing."
    Andrea, 24

♥

"Religiously, you aren't supposed to, but maybe it is a good idea."
    Mark, 73

♥

"Like my ten-year-old cousin said: 'You should find out how good he is in that department before you go any further.'"
    Catherine, 28

IS IT WISE TO LIVE WITH SOMEONE BEFORE MARRIAGE?

"You bet your life it is."
Sheila, 30

♥

"I can't see how it can hurt. If you're not happy before marriage, you won't be happy after."
Scott, 24

♥

"Living together should never be used as a test—it should only happen when two people love each other enough to make a commitment."
Leigh, 37

♥

"Sometimes a little mystery is a good thing."
Hector, 35

"Wisdom is knowing whether or not your love is a forever kind of love. Living together won't tell you that, only your heart can."
    Jackie, 30

♥

"It's wise to know each other intimately; the living together is up to each individual."
    Deon, 32

♥

"If I'm going to go through all the trouble of rearranging my furniture, it might as well be for keeps."
    Debra, 38

♥

"Yes, it is a good idea. Marriage is a big enough adjustment without having to get used to living with that person as well."
    Catherine, 28

CHAPTER III

TRAVELING THE PATH OF LOVE

"And think not you can direct the course of love, for love,
if it finds you worthy, directs your course."
—Kahlil Gibran, *The Prophet*

The road of love may be paved with good intentions, but it is not always smooth. We must stop every now and then to remove some pebbles from the path or step gingerly in order to avoid love's pitfalls. But love can serve as our guide, and if we are true to it, love will lead us around all obstacles and on to safer, if not sacred, ground.

For some of us, love is beyond our control, something bigger and more powerful than we are. Once found, love seems to lead us where *it* wants to go, not where *we* want to go. Love can be confusing and even painful at times as it weaves through our lives; and yet when love is flowing smoothly and effortlessly, there is nothing more uplifting.

As love leads us onward in life, different thoughts and questions arise: How do we deal with the disappointments of love? Do men and women differ in their notions of love and loving behavior?

How can we make love endure? What does loving another person really mean?

To know the triumph and joys of love is to also know the struggles of the heart. But as we examine our life experiences, we also discover with delight that wisdom is also one of the great benefits of loving. While we learn bountifully in the pursuit of love, it is actually in the course of love that the most compelling and transcendent learning takes place.

DO WE LOVE AS DEEPLY WHEN WE ARE YOUNG AS WHEN WE ARE OLDER?

"The trick is to keep vitality in an old relationship and find depth in a young one."
Sherry, 52

♥

"A youthful kiss is like the fleeting brilliance of sunset. A seasoned kiss lingers with the memories of a lifetime of love."
Angel, 52

♥

"Sometimes with the wisdom of age, worries and material concerns recede, and love comes more to the forefront."
Gary, 50

♥

"Young couples can't understand the pure joy of holding hands after forty-five years of marriage. It's a unique pleasure reserved for those who have stood the test of time."
Guy, 70

"Love has to do with the length of the relationship, not necessarily the age of the people involved."

Heather, 22

♥

"The young always look to the future with their relationship . . . The older you get, the more you appreciate your relationship in the present—you value each and every day."

Boyd, 65

♥

"Old lovers understand the magic that Father Time bestows upon a relationship."

Agatha, 67

♥

"When I see an older couple in love, it is as if they share a secret that no one else could possibly understand . . . I see it in the way their eyes sparkle at one another."

Candace, 23

♥

"Love's depth knows no age limit . . . It doesn't give a darn about what you look like, it cares only about what you feel like."

Karl, 39

HOW DOES LOVING YOURSELF INFLUENCE THE WAY YOU LOVE ANOTHER PERSON?

"You have to know love in order to express love."

Eldon, 22

♥

"You can give to someone else only what you have inside your own heart. If your self-love is limited, then all your love is limited."

Regina, 31

♥

"You have to find the beauty in your own soul before you can see and appreciate the beauty in others."

Sheila, 39

"Your greatest love affair should be with yourself . . . If you're going to spend twenty-four hours a day with yourself, you might as well enjoy it."
Michelle, 40

♥

"If you go too far into loving yourself, you can get too self-centered and then you can't love another."
Bernie, 70

♥

"It's hard to break bread with someone else when your own belly is starving and empty."
Hugh, 65

♥

"Some people are dependent on others to tell them they're lovable . . . But if you love yourself, you're already a complete person."
Heather, 22

WHAT ARE SOME OF THE SUREST WAYS TO MAKE LOVE ENDURE?

"Share everything . . . including the laundry, the cooking, and your deepest feelings."
> Marti, 28

♥

"Love endures because you want it to, not by accident. That's the most important thing to remember."
> Roberto, 53

♥

"Carve your names on a tree and put a heart around them. I saw this in a movie and the people stayed together until it said 'The End.'"
> Art, 8

♥

"Put love notes on the refrigerator, and every time you eat you'll think about love and not the moldy vegetables."
> Mary Ellen, 7

"Never lose faith in your love for each other, even when things aren't going well. Try a little harder, let love show you the way."
Betty, 47

♥

"It's all in seeing with your heart . . . If you see your lover's little idiosyncrasies as part of who they are, you'll even love them for squeezing the toothpaste from the top, instead of arguing about it."
Steffie, 24

♥

"When two people really choose in their hearts to go through life together, love will endure."
Seth, 39

♥

"Learn to say these two simple words: 'I'm sorry.'"
Claude, 45

♥

"My grandmother always said: 'Love lasts when you celebrate the little things in life, appreciate the big things, and cook pasta three times a week for dinner—they all make life more delicious.'"
Liz, 29

DO YOU EVER FALL OUT OF LOVE?

"It's like an elastic band—you can only fall out so far and then you bounce back."
    Mike, 18

♥

"Love takes many forms and it can also take flight. Sometimes love just floats away."
    Grant, 35

♥

"Falling out of love is like watching a shooting star fizzle into the darkness. Finding true love is like having the sun rise in your heart and never set."
    John, 75

♥

"To find love you have to do a lot of falling . . . and sometimes you get quite a bump on your head."
    Hank, 65

"Falling out of love is like waking up from a dream—you realize you were only imagining the real thing; you have to clear your head and keep searching."
Gerald, 20

♥

"Real love is not limited by space or time. If you fall out of love, the love you had was but a stepping stone to the real thing."
Marianna, 29

♥

"Love is an eternal feeling . . . genuine love is not something that fades or falls away. Experiences can fade, but love never can."
Fred, 39

♥

"I think falling out of love is like slipping off an old sweater that doesn't fit anymore. You have to find a better-fitting sweater to replace it with."
Marge, 54

WHAT IS THE BEST THING TO DO AFTER A FAILED LOVE AFFAIR?

"Do whatever is going to make you happy—
get a haircut, go on vacation, eat three boxes
of cookies—but then, above all, get on with
your life."
Stacie, 24

♥

"It's OK to retreat into yourself and be sad for a
little while, but then it's important to see your
friends and remind yourself that you're not
alone and forlorn forever."
Heather, 22

♥

"If the fish you caught gets away, find a new
pond and throw in another line."
Ray, 49

"Don't analyze your failed relationship to death
. . . Focus on the positive things you got out of
it and learned from it."
Catherine, 28

♥

"No matter how painful the end of a relationship or marriage might be, eventually you must
find the courage to open yourself up to new
relationships. A life without loving will never
be a full one."
June, 53

♥

"Take some time to heal and then get back on
the horse. But don't make the mistake of riding
the same one that threw you the first time."
Chung, 56

♥

"Cry, see a therapist, talk to your friends—do
whatever is going to bring back your faith in
love and relationships."
Yusef, 39

WHAT HAPPENS TO YOUR FEELINGS OF LOVE WHEN A RELATIONSHIP DOESN'T WORK OUT?

"Making mistakes is what helps us learn about ourselves . . . Don't hate yourself for making a bad choice, just learn to choose better the next time."

Seamus, 33

♥

"You'll never win the game by sitting on the sidelines . . . A few cuts and bruises are part of the struggle to attain your true love. Stay in the game."

Jason, 29

♥

"You can keep them in a secret pocket and save them."

Gayle, 6

"They get recycled. Just discarding your feelings is no good for your immediate environment or your future one."
Nina, 32

♥

"They get written into the book of experience. Then you open a new chapter and try to write a happier, more satisfying story."
Marie, 30

♥

"You don't ever really lose them. You hold onto them as part of a nice memory about that person . . . But you might go through some pain first."
Catherine, 28

♥

"Lost love feelings are like misdirected mail they get returned to sender and then hopefully get readdressed to the correct party."
Nicki, 43

"Each time a relationship doesn't work, that particular love moves over to help make room for the real thing."
    Fred, 39

♥

"I like to think that old love feelings become stars in the sky. When you look up at night, the millions of stars remind you that you are not alone in your search for true love."
    Helena, 31

♥

"You rewrap your love feelings and give them as a gift to someone new, always with the hope that you will receive the gift of their love in return."
    Ernest, 63

DO MEN AND WOMEN SPEAK THE SAME LANGUAGE WHEN IT COMES TO LOVE?

"We all speak the same language, it just sounds funny when men speak it."
    Anna, 17

♥

"Both of them enjoy nonverbal communication the best."
    Nancy, 21

♥

"From my experience in the second grade, girls and boys both like to talk about lovey stuff, but not with each other."
    Carmen, 8

♥

"Men and women speak the same language but with different dialects. You have to find some-one with a dialect you can understand."
    Vivian, 38

"Love is a language of the heart. We can all speak that language if we really want to."
    Colin, 49

♥

"Men and women are different, period. That's what makes life interesting and that's what gives fire and passion to love."
    Ken, 45

♥

"Men and women speak different languages, but love is often the interpreter that brings them together."
    Janet, 53

♥

"Society would have us believe that men and women are destined to live the miserable lives of the people in those TV beer commercials. But I think that most men and women can speak the same language."
    Candi, 30

"Women are more vocal about love. Men like to think you know how they feel without them having to say it."
Toni, 57

♥

"Trying to figure each other out gives men and women something to do on rainy Saturday nights."
Alec, 35

♥

"It all started with Adam and Eve. If they had just tried a little harder to talk over their decision about the apple, then today talking to the opposite sex wouldn't be so controversial."
Hank, 65

♥

"When it comes to love, everyone speaks French."
David, 35

ARE MEN AND WOMEN EQUALLY PASSIONATE WHEN IT COMES TO LOVE?

"Yes, but equal passion doesn't mean there's always equal rights in the relationship."
Cindy, 21

♥

"Men lean more toward sexual expressions of passion, and women lean more toward emotional expressions. But when you're in love, the two melt into one passion that generates a lot of heat."
Kyle, 29

♥

"Yes . . . as long as the man isn't also hopelessly in love with golf."
Vivian, 38

"If you judge by what you see on television, men are driven by animal passion for sex, and women are seductresses whose passion is controlling men with sex. The truth is, we are really passionate about love, because love is why we are here."

Lila, 54

♥

"Men's and women's need for each other is equally passionate; anyone who doesn't believe that is kidding themselves."

Jason, 29

♥

"Men and women have the same feelings on the inside. Something just seems to change when the feelings get converted to words."

Ian, 35

WHAT PERCENTAGE OF A LOVE RELATIONSHIP SHOULD BE SEXUAL?

"A small percentage in terms of building love, a large percentage in terms of sharing love."
Scott, 24

♥

"Forty percent . . . because fifty percent of the time you're out of the house, and the other ten percent you're eating."
Mike, 18

♥

"Sex is like dessert after a hearty meal. It's perfect after you have a balanced love-relationship, but on its own it will leave you feeling hungry and unsatisfied."
Noelle, 29

♥

"Sex is icing on the cake and you can never have too much icing on your cake."
Chloe, 39

"I know a lot of couples who had great sexual relationships, but their marriages ended in divorce. Sex is not what holds a marriage together; it's just a bonus for loving each other in the first place."

Dean, 40

♥

"Sex is fun, but it doesn't wrap its arms around you when you are hurting and comfort you with love . . . Only a loving, caring partner can do that."

Lauren, 25

♥

"Sex isn't necessarily all that it's supposed to be; sometimes it's even better and more important than that."

Al, 42

♥

"A good relationship is one hundred percent love, one hundred percent friendship, and one hundred percent romance . . . You have to give one hundred percent to every aspect of your relationship."

Ron, 53

D<small>O YOU BELIEVE THAT LOVE IS</small>
E<small>TERNAL, OR IS IT SOMETHING</small>
<small>THAT GROWS OUT OF OUR</small>
<small>BIOLOGICAL NEEDS?</small>

"Pizza is a human need; love is the human
quest for eternity."
　　Faith, 18

♥

"Once you say your marriage vows, the love had
better be more than biological or else you're
headed for a lot of pain."
　　Camille, 31

♥

"It's a biological need . . . We all need love to
survive. We need other people to care about or
nothing else really makes sense."
　　Catherine, 28

"Maybe if we could dissect love in my brother's biology class we'd know for sure."
    Frannie, 8

♥

"Love is both eternal and a human need . . . As humans we need love to exist, and as creatures of God, we know love is the journey that leads to forever."
    Artie, 38

♥

"When you've lived as long as I have, you know in your heart that love is beyond what our human minds can comprehend. Only our souls know the true origin and destiny of love."
    Ginny, 71

♥

"One year I didn't get any Valentines and it made me very sad . . . maybe love is like a kid's need to get a Valentine's card, even if it's just a small one."
    Mishelle, 8

"Love is the only human need that exists in both the spiritual and material realms. On Earth, we need food, clothing, shelter, and love to survive. In Heaven, all we need is love."

Ian, 35

CHAPTER IV

HARVEST OF LOVE

"To keep the fire burning brightly there's one easy rule:
Keep the two logs together, near enough to keep each other
warm and far enough apart—about a finger's breadth—for
breathing room. Good fire, good marriage, same rule."
—Marnie Reed Crowel

nce the search is over and you have found love, a new journey has begun. For many, this journey means marriage—that most blissful state of romance that often also leads to years of changing attitudes and changing dirty diapers as well. Marriage is both a spiritual state of being and a constant process of compromise and evolution. When two lives are joined, there is an intricate dance that must be learned and shared. Such a dance often requires couples to practice many rigorous lessons before an effortless waltz is mastered.

Some spouses are quick to point out that marriage is not all wine and roses. But marriage is a commitment to walk the same path, even when the path seems so narrow that the two of you can barely squeeze by. When a marriage is bonded by love and fidelity, there is joy in the constant challenge to evolve both as individuals and as a couple.

There are many concerns to juggle in today's marriages—gender roles, marital communication, finances, two-career families, day care, retirement planning, finding time for yourself, finding time for your friends, your spouse, and your children, and the list goes on and on. As life becomes increasingly hectic, stress on marriage also increases, and the nature of marriage becomes ever more complex. That's all the more reason why acting with a heart filled with love, and not one beleaguered by stress, is so vital to fulfillment in marriage.

Marriage is indeed a noble enterprise. Regardless of how long we have been married, most of us earnestly strive to deepen our love, improve our marriages, and enhance our lives. May the following selections provide you with food for thought.

HOW DO YOU KNOW WHEN YOU ARE READY TO GET MARRIED?

"I heard it's when a guardian angel tells you . . .
Boy, I sure wish that little angel would hurry up
and get the word to me."
Beth, 26

♥

"When the thought of spending the rest of your
life with that person makes you happy."
Scott, 24

♥

"When you both start liking your eggs prepared
the same way."
Leigh, 37

♥

"I knew right away—I felt it in my heart."
Mark, 73

"I met my husband on a Sunday and on Thursday we started talking about getting married . . . You just know."

　　Barbara, 71

♥

"If you already have some gray hairs, then it might be time to listen for wedding bells."

　　Haley, 7

♥

"You know after you have lived with a person and you still feel it's right to be together."

　　Catherine, 28

♥

"We were walking down the street on our first date. We turned the corner and it was like a bolt of lightning hit me. I thought, Wow, he's different from anyone I've ever known. And I knew he was the one."

　　Liz, 29

"When a voice goes off in your soul and says, 'I can be happy with this person.'"
David, 35

♥

"When you get tired of spending your own money, you might want to think about getting married."
Minnie, 7

♥

"When the thought of marrying your lover makes you more excited than scared, then you're ready."
Fred, 39

IS MARRIAGE AN END OR A BEGINNING?

"For some people it's the beginning, for some people it's the end, and for some it's the beginning of the end."
   Blanche, 70

♥

"It is both the end of a search and the beginning of a new one."
   Missy, 29

♥

"It is the end of your childhood and the beginning of your grown-up life."
   Carey, 8

♥

"It's an end to frozen dinners for one and the beginning of home-cooked meals for two."
   Amy, 24

"It means the end of dating lots of girls and the beginning of dating only one for the rest of your life."

Ricky, 9

♥

"It's the beginning with someone you want to go into the future with."

Mark, 73

♥

"Marriage is an end to your loneliness and the beginning of your joy."

Bridget, 35

♥

"Marriage is the beginning of letting go of controls . . . that includes the remote control."

Jeremy, 45

♥

"A good marriage means the end of winter and the beginning of spring."

Mike, 18

WHAT IS THE BIGGEST SURPRISE THAT PEOPLE DISCOVER ABOUT MARITAL LOVE?

"It doesn't take away all your loneliness, but it does give you a companion and friend to talk things out with."
Ellen, 23

♥

"Fun doesn't have to end just because you're married."
Claire, 15

♥

"Every morning you feel blessed because no matter what else might be going wrong, you have each other to love."
Janet, 53

♥

"One lover can really be enough. It really can."
Ted, 25

"You begin to enjoy the way he leaves the refrigerator door open while he drinks from the milk carton, just because you love him so much."
Delia, 32

"Marriage is good for people. It helps the men take naps and it helps the ladies get tough jar lids opened for them."
Terrance, 8

"You're really not married until you share the same bathroom together."
Lucille, 55

"Marriage, if happily maintained, is the greatest and most satisfying reward for having a good set of values and a good heart as well."
Jerome, 44

"It takes more creativity to stay married than it did to think of pickup lines to get dates."
George, 41

♥

"Somebody else is always with you . . . There's no more 'I will do this' or 'I will do that' . . . It's always we."
Bernie, 70

WHAT IS THE NUMBER ONE RULE OF MARRIAGE?

"Never talk about finances after 9 P.M."
Val, 43

♥

"Try to be calm when you disagree . . . Among other things, it's good for your digestive system."
Dinah, 39

♥

"One of the two people has to cook good."
Larry, 9

♥

"Ask not what your wife can do for you, but what you can do for your wife."
Carmine, 35

"Always talk it out."
    Blanche, 70

♥

"Love your spouse as yourself—and then some."
    Molly, 29

♥

"You have to behave . . . Marriage is kind of like kindergarten in that way."
    Juanita, 8

♥

"Don't cheat on each other . . . The penalty for that is death of the relationship."
    Catherine, 28

♥

"Never marry for money."
    Marion, 59

"Have a mutual respect . . . Acknowledge each other . . . If that doesn't happen then the possibility for genuine love is much reduced."
     Bernie, 70

"Don't play games with each other and be as honest as you can."
     Barbara, 71

"Never go to sleep without giving your partner a hug and kiss good-night . . . Even if you're mad at them."
     Lucille, 55

"You have to share everything from toothpaste to tennis rackets, but especially you must share love."
     Natalie, 42

Are good marriages made in Heaven or here on Earth?

"Marriage can be consummated anywhere . . .
But the best ones continue on into Heaven."
Evan, 35

♥

"My parents had their marriage made in Las
Vegas."
Minnie, 7

♥

"They're made by angels that work in the
marriage department in Heaven—but they don't
use express delivery . . . The making of a good
marriage takes time."
Branden, 28

♥

"It's *Bashert*—that is a Hebrew word that means
'this person is meant for me . . . She is my
destiny.'"
Mark, 73

"Souls are made in Heaven and they meet on Earth. But even soul mates can have a failed marriage if they don't work hard at nourishing their love."

Betty, 47

♥

"They're made on Earth . . . but sometimes you have to go through Hell to make them work."

Lucille, 55

♥

"There is a thin veil between what is in Heaven and on Earth . . . Marriage is one way to glimpse what is behind the veil."

Angelica, 29

♥

"Heaven plants love in the heart, and the love is harvested in a good marriage here on Earth."

Christa, 31

♥

"They're made on Earth with two people and a lot of effort."

Scott, 24

WHAT DO ALL GOOD MARRIAGES HAVE IN COMMON?

"Happy children."
   Carey, 8

♥

"Lots of unlimited, unconditional love."
   Vivian, 38

♥

"A nice blend of a modern outlook and old-fashioned values."
   Eva, 58

♥

"A deep and binding friendship."
   Ken, 45

♥

"Humor . . . You have to be able to laugh at yourself and the things that happen to you."
   Barbara, 71

"RESPECT."
    Dean, 40

♥

"Room for each person to make mistakes, learn from them, and grow."
    Jenna, 29

♥

"BALANCE . . . Every great marriage I've seen has a spender and a saver who both know how to compromise."
    Nellie, 82

♥

"Love that can tolerate love handles."
    Dale, 35

♥

"Even after you've been married a long time, in a good marriage you still call each other those special nicknames that have an unspoken 'I love you' attached to them."
    Heather, 22

"Faith."
    Mike, 18

♥

"Partners that actually like each other as people."
    Debra, 38

♥

"A TV that doesn't get used much."
    Elliot, 65

♥

"God is one of the partners in every good marriage."
    Ian, 35

♥

"The only thing good marriages have in common is that they are all different. Each couple constructs their own way to have a good one."
    Bernie, 70

WHERE DO SOME MARRIAGES GO WRONG?

"When a couple forgets what brought them together in the first place."
    Betty, 47

♥

"Some spouses fear change . . . Even good relationships need room for growth and new challenges."
    Anthony, 46

♥

"Marriages can fail over arguments about whether or not the window should be open or closed."
    Bernie, 70

♥

"People start looking for something better outside their marriage, not realizing that they could have that something better in their relationship if they worked at it."
    Lucille, 55

"Sometimes people throw away a lifetime of love for one night of sex . . . Talk it out before you decide to throw it all away."
Lou, 55

♥

"When selfishness rules the home."
Alvin, 35

♥

"When someone wants to stand up at the wedding to say that the two people fight too much to get married . . . That can be a bad sign."
Lina, 9

♥

"When you allow yourself to become a victim of the 'if only' syndrome."
Debra, 38

♥

"When your spouse communicates more effectively at the office than at home, your marriage is in trouble . . . If more people applied their professional communication skills to marriage, there'd be a lot less divorce."
Jackson, 41

WORDS OF WISDOM FOR ANYONE WHO WANTS TO ENHANCE THE LOVE IN THEIR MARRIAGE.

"Remember to stop and smell the roses, and buy them for your wife once in a while."
Angela, 39

♥

"Most families today have two parents working outside the home . . . Between finances and day-to-day problems, there's no time left for the relationship. Make your relationship the number one priority and things will fall into place from there."
Fred, 39

♥

"Forget what anyone else says or what great love is supposed to be . . . Just do it, just love."
Bernie, 70

♥

"Read Song of Solomon out loud to your spouse."
Ian, 35

"Marriage is how two people learn to share."
Kenny, 8

♥

"Do everything opposite of those soap operas—except leave in the kissy stuff."
Melissa, 8

♥

"Breaking up your routine every so often will keep your relationship from cracking."
Jackson, 40

♥

"Marriage isn't what causes divorce; it's forgetting what marriage means that causes divorce."
Dani, 32

♥

"Do what you can to make your partner happy and it will be reciprocated."
Scott, 24

♥

"After you tie the knot, make sure you don't pull so hard that you turn your marriage into a tug-of-war."
Helene, 27

"Marriage is like having an old Mercedes . . .
You have to give it constant, loving care and
regular tune ups and then have faith it will go
the distance with you."

Pedro, 45

♥

"Do something crazy and spontaneous to
remind yourself of the 'good old days.'"

Andrea, 24

♥

"You have to expect some clouds and rain in
every marriage, or else you'd never see a rainbow."

Gina, 32

♥

"Have a date night—once a month where you
spend the evening or weekend together, alone."

Lucille, 55

♥

"Say those three special words constantly . . .
It's not 'Love ya, Babe,' but really say 'I love
you.'"

B.K., 70

IS MARITAL LOVE MORE OF AN ART, OR SOMETHING WITH SKILLS YOU CAN LEARN?

"Every marriage is like a work of art, and the world is like a museum. Some of the artwork you will like and learn from, and some will make you wonder how it ever got into a museum in the first place."

George, 41

♥

"Everyone can love . . . but it is only through the act of loving that we can learn to love more fully."

Anita, 29

♥

"I think you can learn it—that's how the chocolate makers keep their secret recipes for Valentine's Day candies going."

Terrie, 8

"Love is a creative gift God gave to us all . . .
But some people work harder at improving this
gift than others."

Angie, 40

♥

"If making mistakes and apologizing is a skill
you can learn, then marriage is the art of perfecting that skill."

Ben, 35

♥

"Marital love is something you can learn . . .
People can always change if they want to. They
can learn understanding and patience. But you
can't learn trust—that just has to be there."

Catherine, 28

♥

"Love is like art because it makes you feel
creative all over."

Alisha, 13

"Love doesn't come with a how-to manual . . .
You have to make it work by using whatever
skills you've picked up along the way. After a
while, you either catch on or let go."

Betsy, 27

♥

"Love is not the complicated mess that a lot of
book writers and movie makers would have us
believe it is . . . Love is as natural to the human
race as rain is to flowers."

Hank, 65

♥

"God gave us the gift of love . . . Loving our
spouse and children is our creative gift to God.
Returning the love unused would be a tremen-
dous insult."

Mary, 64

♥

"Love is an art . . . Our nervousness about it
comes from knowing that we are sculpting our
relationship with our own two hands."

Pablo, 31

WHAT ARE THE REASONS WHY SOME PEOPLE HAVE DIFFICULTY WITH MONOGAMY?

"The person might be too hung up on phrases like 'the more the merrier.'"
  Garin, 33

♥

"True intimacy is too scary."
  Debra, 38

♥

"It's a way of keeping distance from long-term relationships . . . a definite way of saying 'I'm still separate from you.'"
  Heather, 22

♥

"Variety is the spice of life, but it's best to have one spicy wife."
  Nathan, 31

"Some lovers are greedy—they take what they have for granted and want what they don't have."

Scott, 24

♥

"Some people lack self esteem and feel unattractive, so the more people they are with the better they feel about themselves."

Catherine, 28

♥

"They might be afraid of having what they really want, so they sabotage the relationship by sleeping with someone else."

Isaac, 35

♥

"I think life is much simpler if you only have to buy Valentine's gifts for one girl at a time . . . and it's cheaper, too."

Jess, 12

WHEN IN A MARRIAGE DO YOU KNOW THAT YOUR LOVE IS SUFFICIENT TO BRING A CHILD INTO THE WORLD?

"When the marriage boat isn't rocking back and forth, you're ready to rock a baby in your arms."
Kendra, 35

♥

"When the thought of taking care of someone else doesn't panic you."
Catherine, 28

♥

"It's a decision you should make before you get married. You don't want to find out later that you want children and your spouse doesn't."
Lucille, 55

"Sometimes a child is unexpected—that's when you realize that love multiplies as easily as people do."
Agatha, 55

♥

"In general, if you're not ready to talk about it and agree about it, then you're not ready for children."
Bernie, 70

♥

"When you are happy with yourself and your marriage and yet you still feel there is something missing in your life, it might be time to invest in Pampers."
Louise, 36

WHAT WILL YOU TELL YOUR CHILDREN OR GRANDCHILDREN ABOUT ROMANTIC LOVE?

"Wait until the fourth grade to go steady—by then you'll have love all figured out."
Danny, 9

♥

"Never underappreciate love when you find it."
Scott, 24

♥

"Love is more fun than horseshoes and at least a little bit safer than hang gliding."
Sean, 33

♥

"Marriage is the best thing that can happen to you—and the most challenging."
David, 35©

"A good marriage is like the ocean—the tide goes out and the tide rolls in; but no matter how long the tide is out, you know it will come back again toward you."

Lucille, 55

♥

"Love generously, but wisely."

Lisette, 21

♥

"Go slow. Be sure. Love is like a waltz, not a speedway—you should enjoy and savor each step of the dance."

Debra, 38

♥

"It is truly better to have loved and lost then never to have loved at all—even when it hurts like hell."

James, 44

"Real love keeps you feeling young."
Blanche, 70

♥

"Even if you read all the romance novels you can get your hands on, you aren't prepared for love until you get out of the library and write your own book on the subject."
Jessie Ann, 21

CHAPTER V

THE GLORY OF LOVE

"If I have prophetic powers, and understand all mysteries
and have all knowledge, and if I have all faith so to move
mountains, but have not love, I am nothing."
—I Corinthians 13:1–7

ove has been discussed by poets, philosophers, great thinkers, novelists, artists, clergy, and the common person alike. Because love touches all of our lives, we each have something to contribute—an important piece of the puzzle—when it comes to the wonderful enigma we call love.

Love is at once as old as the world and as young as a newborn child. We each have the interesting task of seeking and giving love and, in so doing, finding ourselves and our life's work and purpose. Love must be our common cornerstone as we build the foundation of our lives.

The more we discover about love, the more questions arise. How does love fit into the greater scheme of things? What does love teach us? Does love really heal all things? What role does love have in our lives? In the pursuit of love's answers, sharing our understanding of love is very important, for we can all help each other find those answers.

Here, we conclude with some of the practical applications of our inquiry into love. We are reminded that as lofty a notion as love may seem at times, it is essentially a living and breathing presence in our lives. As the theologian and modern writer Peter Kreeft has observed, "Love is to the soul what food is to the body." In sharing ideas about love, and in loving one another, we provide for each other what is essential to our happiness—faith in the nature of love and the belief that love does, in fact, conquer all our doubts and fears.

LOVE
MEANS . . .

"Love means always saying you're sorry . . .
especially after you say something negative."
   Sandra, 22

♥

"Love means never yelling over spilled milk—
even if it gets spilled on you."
   Ava, 45

♥

"Love means agreeing to a twelve-hour train
ride because your wife is afraid to fly."
   Marie, 30

♥

"Love means that *I* has been asked to move
over to make room for *we*."
   James, 30

♥

"Love means having faith that your relationship
is strong enough for both tender moments and
tough ones."
   Margaret, 32

"Love means criticism is a four-letter word."
David, 35

♥

"Love means you don't need a rainy day as an excuse to linger in bed—love is excuse enough."
Liz, 29

♥

"Love means giving your friend your milk money because they forgot theirs."
Debbie, 7

♥

"Love means knowing that sometimes you have to hold on and sometimes you have to let go."
Karen, 33

♥

"Love means you don't mind when your dog licks your face because he loves you—it's the love part that counts, not the slobber."
Lu, 8

♥

"Love means that together you have found the power to move mountains."
Amelia, 39

ARE PEOPLE TOO FOCUSED ON ROMANTIC LOVE AS COMPARED TO OTHER TYPES OF LOVE?

"Romantic love is only one of the many kinds of fruitful love that can be abundant in our lives . . . It's like going to the refrigerator for an apple and finding only an orange—it may not be exactly what you think you want, but it will still taste juicy and sweet."

Alberto, 53

♥

"It can't always be hearts and flowers . . . If you don't have something to see you through the times without hearts and flowers, you don't have much."

Debra, 38

♥

"The love of a friend can be as powerful and fulfilling as a romantic love."

John, 75

"Romantic love is fake love—the Hollywood version with stars in your eyes; real love is down-to-earth."

Barbara, 71

♥

"Love, romantic or otherwise, is not what we are constantly bombarded with in the media. Love comes from within, not from wearing Calvin Klein underwear."

Jackson, 41

♥

"If you think all you need in your life is the perfect romance, you will never find true happiness. Joy lies in finding love in your friends, your neighbors, your co-workers, the homeless, and the poor. We need all kinds of love to be fulfilled."

Ginny, 71

♥

"As a society we need to focus on what kind of love we can bring to the world, not what kind of love we can take from it."

Ian, 35

"What society should focus on is being kind, caring, and forgiving toward each other . . . That's the kind of love everyone needs."
Betty, 47

♥

"If you want to know what true love is, turn off the soaps and watch a couple who've been married for fifty years instead."
Nellie, 82

♥

"Grown-ups think about kissing and stuff too much . . . Kids know it's better to have a friend you can trade baseball cards with than it is to have a friend you gotta kiss!"
Jimmy, 8

ON LOVE AND RELIGION . . .

"Love is how God gets people to pay attention
to the important things in life."
   Vivian, 38

♥

"No one will ever need to say, 'Forgive me,
Father, for I have loved.'"
   Lyle, 40

♥

"When you fall in love, it really does give you
the feeling that there is something more powerful and wonderful in the universe."
   Julie, 34

♥

"God is really big on love . . . It says so in His
Book."
   Randi, 7

"A kiss is like a prayer. Each is offered with the hope that it will be answered, and it's a wonderful feeling if that happens."
Maxine, 30

♥

"You don't have to be religious to fall in love, but you can't help noticing that there is a hint of the eternal about the whole thing."
Fran, 40

♥

"You shouldn't turn love into a religion in itself; our focus in life is learning to love, not learning to worship love."
Judy, 42

♥

"I don't know if love can be shallow. I do know that a loving marriage can't be."
Wendy, 29

"Love is the glue that bonds this life to the next. The more love you spread, the greater sense you have of the spiritual."

Jim, 59

♥

"Love must be related to God, because both go on forever."

Fran, 40

♥

"You should go about love religiously; half-hearted efforts at love do not last."

Carolyn, 51

DOES LOVE HEAL ALL THINGS?

"Love is the best therapist I have ever come across."
>   Ian, 35

♥

"Love can heal many things, but it can hurt quite a bit as well."
>   Scott, 24

♥

"No . . . but it makes a hell of a Band-Aid."
>   Debra, 38

♥

"Love can conquer mountains as well as ant hills."
>   Sara, 61

"Love is an elixir you don't need a prescription for."

Ben, 32

♥

"It depends on whether or not you know how to love. If you don't know how to love, you can't use love to heal."

Catherine, 28

♥

"Love and time are the true healers of our pain."

Marie, 30

TO LOVE SOMEONE IS TO . . .

"Risk all your feelings for a very good cause."
Patricia, 18

♥

"Give without a moment's hesitation, for just
the chance that you could better the life of
your lover."
Scott, 24

♥

"Put the needs of your lover above your own."
Betty, 47

♥

"There is no greater act of love than to spend
your life teaching others how to do it."
Marion, 57

"To love someone is to open your eyes to the beauty of life and open your heart to the joys of Heaven."

Darren, 35

♥

"To love someone is to know that your life has substance."

Sophia, 29

♥

"To truly love someone is to know that they will always be a part of you—even after this life is over."

Ginny, 71

WHAT IS THE FUNDAMENTAL THING A PERSON NEEDS TO KNOW ABOUT LOVE?

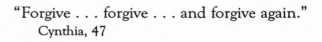

"Forgive . . . forgive . . . and forgive again."
Cynthia, 47

♥

"Don't try to control love. It can't be done."
Marv, 42

♥

"Love conquers all the dumb relationships you had before the real one."
Wendy, 29

♥

"You can be all lovey no matter how old you are."
Harlon, 12

♥

"Don't cling."
Amy, 24

"Grab it when it comes and fight like heck to keep it."

Scott, 24

♥

"Marriage is like running a marathon . . . You know there will be times when you feel like quitting, but you have to have endurance to reap the rewards of staying in the race."

Brenton, 40

♥

"Loving and being loved is good for your health."

Ava, 45

♥

"It doesn't matter if you are going to the grocery store together or going out dancing, it still takes two to tango."

Denise, 33

♥

"Love isn't always easy. Sometimes it hurts, but it's still worth it."

Liz, 29

"Love is an itch around your heart that you can't scratch."
Blanche, 70

♥

"Love isn't the most vital thing; it's the only thing."
Arnold, 48

♥

"Love is like sunshine. You might be able to get along without it for a little while, but it's impossible to live life unless you are touched by love."
Alexia, 30

♥

"Love is like a good book. You've got to read it thoughtfully—not use it to prop up a sofa."
Mike, 18

WHAT DOES LOVE TEACH A PERSON?

"How to ride a bicycle-built-for-two and not fall off."

    Lauren, 25

♥

"Love taught me that I still got a lot to learn about it."

    Howie, 10

♥

"Love teaches you how to wait for the bathroom to be free and not mind the waiting."

    Betty, 47

♥

"Love flows like a stream . . . Even when a rock is in its path, it just keeps right on flowing."

    Lucille, 55

"Love is the best teacher, but not all pupils are ready for its lessons."
Mary, 40

♥

"Love teaches us that love isn't the great question of life . . . it's the one and only answer."
Sallie, 44

♥

"You learn that love comes in so many flavors."
Heather, 22

♥

"You can learn a lot from love because it compels you to ask: Who am I? Where am I going?"
Alexia, 32

♥

"Love teaches you self-respect and respect for others. It gives us courage that we can make the world a better place."
Catherine, 28

"It teaches you to whistle for no special reason."
Jason, 29

♥

"Love teaches us the greatest lessons of life: Love is why we are here, love is our purpose for living, and love is our final destination."
Liz, 29

THE END

143

About the Author

Elizabeth Heller, M.S., is a graduate of Santa Clara University, where she earned a B.A. in English; she holds a master's degree in Broadcast Journalism from Boston University.

She has co-authored several books with her husband, David Heller, including *The Best Christmas Presents Are Wrapped in Heaven* and *Grandparents Are Made for Hugging* (Villard Books). She has also authored *A Kid's Book of Prayers About All Sorts of Things*.

At the same time, Elizabeth Heller has held several media positions, including director of Public Relations for Catholic Charities, director of Research for World Monitor News, and producer, writer, and on-air talent for "Kid Company," a radio program on WBZ-AM in Boston.

Originally from California, Elizabeth Heller lives in Boston with her husband and collaborator, David.